The Origin of Art and Painting

Lazar Popoff

The Origin of Art and Painting

LM Publishers

The Origin of Art

We are accustomed to say that Egypt is the cradle of the arts; yet archaeologists have demonstrated that the earliest works of art are of epochs far anterior to the ancient Egyptian civilizations. According to these authors, these works were contemporaneous with the presence of the reindeer in the south of France, and of a time when the mammoth had not yet disappeared, and when man, ignorant of the metals, made all his instruments of stone, wood, and bone. In reality, the first works of art, particularly the first efforts at drawing, date from prehistoric times. In France they are found in caverns by the side of the fossil remains of animals now extinct, like the mammoth, or which have abandoned those regions, like the reindeer, in the shape of drawings engraved with flint points as decorations of articles of reindeer horn, such as dagger handles and clubs. Drawings have also been observed on tablets of stone, horn, or ivory derived from mammoth's teeth.

We do not intend to dwell on the rudimentary, merely outline drawings, of which these ornaments consist. We invite special attention to more perfect and more characteristic works, in which, as Carl Vogt remarks, the spirit of observation and imitation of Nature, especially of living Nature, is remarkably manifest. The figure of the mammoth attracts our notice at once. A drawing found in the cavern of *La Magdelaine,* in the Dordogne, engraved on a tablet of mammoth bone, is marked by the strikingly clumsy attitude of the unwieldy body of the animal, by its long hair, the form of its lofty skull with concave front, and its enormous recurved tusks. All these features, characteristic of this extinct type of pachyderm, have been reproduced by the designer with a really artistic accuracy. The mammoth was already rare in Europe when this primitive artist lived; and that, perhaps, is the reason why only two among the numerous drawings found in the caverns of France are of that animal. The second of these drawings, which was found in *La Lozère,* is a mammoth's head sculptured on a club.

The figures of the chamois, the bear, and the ox occur more frequently; but those of the reindeer are most numerous. Some are engraved on plates of bone, others as ornaments of various articles. Sometimes groups of animals are represented; or, on the other hand, only parts of them are given, and we see simply the head, or the head and bust.

The large majority of these drawings are no better executed than those which school children make on walls. The figures of the reindeer, however, are superior, by the remarkable care with which the characteristic lines of the animal are traced, and also, in rare specimens, by the addition of shadows. The drawings of the chamois, the bear, and the ox are likewise often strikingly exact and of real value.

Besides these drawings of mammals, several representations of fishes, exact but very uniform, have been found in caverns in France. As a whole, as Broca remarks, all these relics of primitive art demonstrate that the men of this prehistoric period carefully observed the forms and attitudes of animals, and were capable of representing them exactly and elegantly, attesting a real artistic sense.

No such skill has been observed with reference to the representation of the human figure; and designs in which it appears are extremely rare. Of two of them, one represents a man naked, armed with a club, and surrounded by animals; and the second, a fishing scene, in which a man is lancing a harpoon at some marine animal—a fish, according to Broca; a whale, according to others. In this piece we are most interested in the man. The drawing, as a whole, is puerile and deformed, and the proportions are surprisingly violated. The specimen is not an exception, for the examination of all the drawings of this kind proves that the men of those times, while very skillful in the representation of animals, especially of those which were important to them, were very poor delineators of the human figure.

Another not less characteristic point is the complete absence of drawings of plants. No representation of a tree, or bush, or even of a flower is found, unless we regard as of that character the three little rosettes engraved on a handle of reindeer horn, which some authors think is the figure of a composite flower. Such undoubted exclusiveness on the part of the inhabitants of the caves was evidently not accidental, for chance explains nothing; and we cannot admit, with Carl Vogt, that primitive drawing originated in a general tendency of man to the imitation of living Nature. We think the object of these artistic productions was of a quite different character, and that they were originally designed, not for ornament or for pure and simple imitation of Nature, but to secure an instrument for use in the struggle with Nature.

We remark, first, that there is nothing to prove that the men of that epoch were mentally superior to modern savages; and, if we observe these, we shall ascertain that their drawings have usually a very different significance from what they have among civilized peoples, and nothing in common with decoration and æsthetics in general. Numerous facts prove that human thought in the lower stages of its development distinguishes poorly between subjective representations and objective results, and that both give rise to the same ideas. For instance, a savage seeing one of his family in a dream cannot imagine that the image is independent of the organic substance of the personage in question; and he will see the same relation between the two as between a body and its image reflected from the surface of the water. Thus the Basutos think that if the shadow of a man is projected upon the water the crocodiles will obtain possession of the man. A similar identification may be pushed to the point that some tribes are known which use the same word to designate the soul, the image, and the shadow. This is the essential fact to be taken into consideration in order to regard primitive design in its real meaning, and to restore the conditions of the medium in which it originated. If we suppose such a material relation between the image and the object as there is between the shadow and the object, it becomes evident that the savage should deport himself in the same way toward the image, the shadow, and the object. From his point of view the image and the object it represents are in close relation, and in acting upon the one he would be acting in the same way upon the other. By virtue of this way of thinking the savage is convinced that harm done to the image passes to the object, or that in acting upon the copy we attack the original.

Proofs are numerous to demonstrate the importance which savages attribute to this mode of action on the original. Waitz tells, following Denghame, that it was dangerous in a certain tribe of West Africa to paint the portraits of natives, because they were afraid that a part of their soul would pass, by some necromancy, into the image. Sir John Lubbock notices the fear of their portrait entertained by savages—and the more like the portrait, the greater the danger to the original was supposed to be. Dr. Kane got rid of the Indians one day when they were making themselves troublesome to him by beginning to paint their portraits. Catlin relates an incident, at the same time sad and comic, of his drawing the profile of a chief named Matochiga, when the Indians around him seemed all at once very much moved. "Why did you not draw the other half of his face?" they asked; "Matochiga was never ashamed to look a white man in the face." Matochiga did not appear to have taken offense till then, when one of the Indians came up to him and, laughing, said, "The Englishman knows very well that you are only half a man, and he has only drawn half of your face because the other is worth nothing." A fatal quarrel followed this expression, and Matochiga was killed by a bullet which struck him on the side of the face that had not been drawn.

Charlevoix says that the Illinois and other Indian tribes made little figures representing persons whose lives they wished to curtail, and stabbed them in the place of the heart. A custom still exists in Borneo of making a figure in wax of an enemy whom one desires to bewitch and melting it before the fire. They say that the person designated will waste away as his image disappears. Peruvian sorcerers proceed in the same way, except that their figures are made of rags. In the East Indies, according to Dubois, they knead with hair or bits of skin, earth collected in some muddy place, of which they make a figure, on the breast of which they write the name of an enemy; then stab the figure with needles, or otherwise mutilate it—always in the belief that similar injuries will be inflicted upon the person represented.

Vestiges of this primitive superstition are furthermore found among civilized peoples; for, as Grimm relates, Jews were accused, in the eleventh century, in Europe, of having slain Bishop Ebergard by the aid of witchcraft of this kind. These Jews had each a figure of wax representing the bishop, had bribed a priest to baptize it, and had then thrown it in the fire. The wax had hardly melted when the bishop was struck with mortal illness.

The famous adventurer Jacob, chief of the Pastoureaux, who lived in the thirteenth century, believed seriously, as he says in his Demonology, that the devil taught men the art of making images of wax and clay, the destruction of which involved the death of the persons whom they represented. In the time of Catherine de Medicis it was a custom to make such figurines of wax and to melt them over a slow fire, or stab them with needles, in order to make their enemies suffer. The operation was called *envoûtement* (or spell-binding).

We shall not be done unless we cite all the facts that prove that in the mind of the primitive man it is enough to possess any object—a piece of a coat, hair, a bit of a nail—that has belonged to a person to have power to act on him and do him harm. Faith in the efficiency of this means is so strong among backward peoples that persons who have any reason to suspect others hide their clothes in order that no part of them may be stolen. Others, when they cut their hair or nails, put the cut parts on the roof of their house or bury them. So peasants in some countries do with extracted teeth. We add, to complete our picture, that writing is regarded by the savage as endowed with the same magic force as drawing—a fact we may easily comprehend if we recollect that picture-writing preceded writing with letters or any conventional signs, and is still practiced among some savage tribes. In these picture-writings the subjection of a man or an animal to bad luck is indicated by an arrow drawn from the mouth to the heart. A sign of that kind is supposed to be equivalent to a real taking possession of the animal or the person represented.

It is doubtful whether we could give more evident proofs of the entirely special significance attributed by the savage to drawing, regarded by him as an instrument of power over another. While the examples we have cited relate particularly to man, it is logical to assume that the same process—that is, the figurative representation of animals— plays a like part in the struggle of the savage against his natural enemies. There exist other facts that confirm this hypothesis.

According to Mr. Tanner, the North American Indians, to assure success in their hunts, made rude drawings of the animals they pursue, with arrows sticking through the place of the heart, believing that they will by this means obtain power to cause the game they seek to fall into their hands. The Australians, according to an observer quoted by Tylor, make a figure of the kangaroo of grass in order to become the masters of the real kangaroos in the bush. When an Algonkin Indian wanted to slay an animal, he made a grass figure of it and hung it up in his lodge. Then, having named it several times, he shot an arrow at the image. If he hit it, it was a sign that he would kill the animal on the morrow.

In the same way, if the hunter, after he had touched the wand of a wizard with his arrow, strikes the track of an animal with the same arrow, the animal will be stopped in its flight and held till the hunter can catch up with it. The same result, according to the aborigines, can be easily secured by drawing the figure of the animal on a piece of wood, and praying to the image for success in the hunt.

Here, then, we have, in substance, the origin of the part played by drawing. An Indian song expresses this part admirably in the words, "My picture makes a god of me," and it is really doubtful whether faith in the powerful significance of the art of drawing as an instrument by the aid of which primitive man could obtain a supernatural power over his enemy or his game could be more powerfully expressed.

If we now consider the works of the cave men in the light of these facts, we shall recognize that the object that inspired them had really few points in common with the sense of beauty or the tendency to imitation; and it is clear that if there existed in the mind of primitive man a material relation between a being and its shadow or its image, that man would believe that the same relation was preserved between that being and its image transferred to any object. The purpose sought was to possess one's self of the shadow of the desired object, and the only way of doing that was to fix the silhouette of the shadow on some article. This, in our opinion, was the primary purpose of drawing, and consequently of painting.

It is noteworthy that all works of this kind appertaining to the embryonal period of the arts of design display the want of proportionality, the absence of symmetry characteristic of silhouettes of shadows. The uniform impression given by these drawings is that they refer, not to the objects themselves, but to their shadows. It is likewise interesting to remark that some contemporaneous savages—some Australians, for example—are still incapable of grasping the meaning of the most perfectly faithful images, while they readily understand a rude, ill-proportioned drawing. Thus, to give them the idea of a man, he must be drawn with a greatly enlarged head—a detail, the spirit of which is paralleled upon a drawing found in a cavern in France, and representing a fisherman. He has a very small body, but his hand, armed with an enormous harpoon, is the hand of a giant.

In his struggle with surrounding Nature—a struggle of which it is almost impossible for us to conceive an exact idea—the first need of primitive man was to possess some means of giving him confidence in victory. In going to the hunt he took with him, as the North American Indian does, and as do under another form some of the gamblers in our most civilized circles, the fetich that was to assure his success—that is, the image of the animal he wanted to kill. In engraving on the handle of his dagger the likeness of a reindeer or other animal, he was not thinking of decorating his weapon, but only of bringing some magic power to bear upon his prey; and it was precisely faith in that mysterious force, by giving him boldness, energy, and security of movement, that would procure him success. Confidence acts thus in everything.

Like the modern savage, the man of the caves believed that the greater the resemblance between the animal and its likeness, the greater was the chance of acting on the animal. Hence the care taken in the pictured reproduction of animals particularly sought for, and against which his struggle was the most earnest; hence those perfect drawings of the reindeer, that magnificent game of our ancestors. Very different are the characteristics of the drawings of human forms. To account for these differences, it must be considered that all the archæological data relative to the epoch of the reindeer are unanimous in attesting that the man of that age was of a peaceful character.

While, then, we are justified in believing that the men of the caverns very rarely raised their hands against one another, it is none the less certain that they led a bitter and truceless struggle against animals. They therefore rarely had occasion to practice the drawing of the human figure; whence the great imperfections of the figures of that kind as compared with the figures of animals.

It may be remarked, with reference to plant forms, that the boreal flora of that epoch, not being at all menacing, could furnish little food for superstition, and no drawings of plants are found in the caves.

On the whole, the condition of the art of design with primitive man appears to be in complete harmony with the meaning we have attributed to design itself—it being regarded as inspired by the belief in the existence of a material relation between a being and its image, and in the possibility of acting on the object by means of the picture.

Consequently, the principle of painting is not to be found in a natural tendency of primitive man to the artificial imitation of living Nature, but seems to be derived from the wish to subject that Nature to its wants and to subdue it.

By progressive improvements, the art of drawing has gradually lost its primitive significance and original meaning till it has become what it is now. It does not differ, however, much from what it was originally; for, while primitive man fancied he could reach the living being in its image, it is still life that living man seeks today in works of art.

The Origin of Painting

It is said repeatedly, as of course, that Egypt was the cradle of the arts. Yet archaeologists like Lartet, Garrigue, Cristi, and others have shown that the first artistic manifestations go back to epochs far anterior to the ancient Egyptians. According to these authors, these first manifestations were contemporary with the presence of the reindeer in the south of France—when the mammoth had not yet quite disappeared, and when man, ignorant of the metals, made all his instruments of stone, bone, and wood. In fact, the first works of art, and particularly the first efforts at drawing, date from those prehistoric times. In France, the oldest remains of these works of art have been found, in the shape of drawings engraved with a flint point as ornaments on articles of reindeer-horn, in caves by the side of the fossil remains of animals which, like the mammoth, have since disappeared, or, like the reindeer, have abandoned those regions. Other drawings have been found on tablets of stone, horn, or mammoth-ivory.

It is not our intention to insist on the simply linear rudimentary designs of which these ornaments consist. We rather invite attention to more perfect and characteristic works, in which, according to the words of Carl Vogt, the spirit of observation and imitation of Nature, and especially of living Nature, is remarkably manifested. An image of a mammoth, found in the cave of La Magdelaine, in the Dordogne, is engraved on a tablet of mammoth-bone. Very striking are the ungainly attitude of the animal's massive body, its long hair, the form of its elevated skull, with concave forehead, and its enormous recurved tusks. All these traits, characteristic of this extinct type of pachyderm, are reproduced by the designer with a really artistic distinctness. The mammoth was already rare in Europe when this primitive artist lived; and this, perhaps, is the reason why only two of the numerous designs found in the caves of France are of this animal. –The second of these drawings, found in La Lozère, represents a mamoth's head sculptured on a staff of command. The images of the chamois, bear, and ox are found more frequently; hut figures of the reindeer are most numerous. Some are engraved on plates of bone, and others serve to ornament various objects. Sometimes groups of animals are represented, or, on the other hand, the animals are only partly drawn, and merely the head or head and chest are visible.

The larger part of these drawings do not excel in execution the figures which our school-boys make on walls; but the figures of the reindeer are generally superior on account of the remarkable care with which the characteristic lines of the animal are traced, and also, in examples that are otherwise very rare, by the addition of a few shadows. We conclude that the artist of the caves was particularly interested in the reindeer, which furnished his contemporaries with their principal food, as well as with clothing materials, arms for hunting, and household implements. We know, in fact, that the cave-dwellers lived on reindeer-meat, dressed themselves in its skin, made thread of its tendons, and cut their arrow-points from its bones. In other words, as the reindeer had not yet been domesticated, it stood to those primitive men as a valuable game, and the hunting of it occupied the larger part of their existence. We thus explain why that animal haunted the imagination of the artist of those times. The drawings of the chamois, the bear, and the ox were also often surprisingly exact and really valuable.

Besides these designs of mammals, there have been found in the caves of France a number of drawings of fishes, tolerably correct, but very uniform. According to Broca, they can all be referred to the salmon.

All these relics of the primitive arts of design prove abundantly that the men of that prehistoric age observed carefully the forms and attitudes of animals and were capable of representing them in an exact and elegant style, attesting, according to Broca, a real artistic sense.

Nothing like this has been observed in the reproduction of the human figure, and drawings of that kind are extremely rare. There are two such deserving mention, one of which represents a naked man, armed with a club and surrounded by animals; the second, a fishing scene, a man lancing a harpoon upon a marine animal—a fish according to Broca, a whale according to other authors. The whole of the design is puerile and out of shape, and the proportions are outrageously violated. This is not an exception, for the examination of all the drawings of this kind shows that skillful as were the men of those times in their drawings of animals, particularly of those which were important to them, they were bad delineators of the human figure. "I do not know," says Broca, "what prevented them from reaching perfection on this point, but the fact is indisputable and is certainly characteristic." Another no less characteristic point is the entire absence of designs representing plants. No design of a tree has been found, or of a bush or a flower, unless we regard as a flower the "three little rosettes" engraved on a handle of reindeer-horn, which some authors actually regard as a composite flower. This exclusive taste of the artists of the caves is evidently not accidental, for chance explains nothing; and we can not assume, with Carl Vogt, that primitive drawing originated in a general tendency of man toward imitation of living Nature. "We believe that the object of these artistic productions was of a different character, and that they were intended, not for ornamentation of objects or for imitation pure and simple of Nature, but for the production of an instrument to be used in the struggle against Nature. We shall endeavor to substantiate this proposition in what follows, and shall have occasion to say something on the origin of painting in general.

We remark, first, that there is nothing to prove that the man of that time was intellectually superior to existing savages; and, if we observe these, we shall find that their drawings have usually a totally different significance from that which art has among civilized peoples; and that they have nothing in common with ornamentation and æsthetics in general. Indeed, numerous facts go to show that human thought, in the lower degrees of its development, distinguishes but poorly between subjective representations and objective reality, and that both give rise to the same ideas. For example, a savage seeing one of his family in a dream, cannot imagine that the image is independent of the organic substance of the person in question; and he will see the same relation between the two as between a body and its image reflected by a surface of water. Thus the Basutos believe that if the shadow of a man is projected upon the water, the crocodiles will be able to seize the man himself. A like identification may be pushed to the point that tribes are known which use the same word for the soul, the image, and the shadow.

It is necessary to take this fact into consideration in order to appreciate the real sense of the primitive design, and to re-establish the conditions under which it originated. If we suppose a material relation between the image and the object as well as between the shadow and the object, it becomes evident that the savage would comport himself similarly toward the image, the shadow, and the object. From his point of view the image and the object are in close relation, and an action upon one wonld operate in the same way upon the other. By this way of looking at things, as Sir John Lubbock says, the savage is convinced that an injury done to the image is inflicted upon the original; or, to use the words of Mr. Taylor, he thinks that by acting upon the copy he will reach the original. The evidences are many that demonstrate the importance attributed by savages to this mode of action on the original.

Waitz relates, after Denghame, that in a tribe of western Africa it was dangerous to make a portrait of the natives, because they were afraid that by some kind of sorcery a part of their soul would pass into their image. Lubbock also speaks of the same fear as existing among savages; and the more like the portrait, the greater the danger to the original; for the more life there is in the copy, the less must be left in the person. One day, when some Indians were annoying Dr. Kane by their presence, he rid himself of them very quickly by telling them that he was going to make their portraits. Catlin tells a story, at once sober and comical, that when he was drawing the profile of a chief named Matochiga, the Indians around him seemed greatly moved, and asked him why he did not draw the other half of the chiefs face. "Matochiga was never ashamed to look a white man square in the face." Matochiga had not till then seemed offended at the matter, but one of the Indians said to him sportively: "The Yankee knows that you are only half a man, and he has only drawn half of your face, because the other half is not worth anything." A bloody fight followed this explanation, and Matochiga was killed by a bullet which struck him in the side of the face that had not been drawn. A still more characteristic incident is communicated by M. Brouck concerning a Laplander who had come to visit him from motives of curiosity. He having drunk a glass of wine and seeming very much at ease, M. Brouck took his pencil and began drawing his portrait. All at once our subject's humor changed; he drew on his cap and started to run away. Explanations being had, the Laplander made the rash artist understand that, if he had let him copy his figure, the artist would have gained a dangerous influence over him.

Charlevoix said, in the last century, that the Illinois and Indians of some other tribes made little figures representing persons whose lives they wanted to shorten, and pierced them in the region of the heart. A custom still exists in Borneo that consists in making a figure in wax of the enemy whom one wishes to bewitch, and setting it before the fire to melt; it is assumed, according to Taylor, that the person aimed at is disorganized as fast as his image disappears. The Peruvian sorcerers still proceed in the same way, except that their figures are made of rags. In the Indies, according to Dubois, they knead earth collected from a very salt place with hair or pieces of skin, and make a figure on the chest of which they write the name of an enemy, and then stab it with needles, or mutilate in some way, in the belief that the same harm will be suffered by the person represented.

Traces of this primitive superstition are also found among civilized people, for Grimn reports that in the eleventh century Jews were accused in Europe of having killed Bishop Ebergard by a sorcery of the kind. They were said to have made a figure of wax representing the bishop, hired a priest to baptize it, and put it into the fire. As soon as the wax was melted, the bishop was attacked by a mortal disease. The famous adventurer, Jacob, chief of the Pastorals, in the thirteenth century, seriously believed, as he says in his Demonology, that the devil taught men the art of making images of wax and clay, the destruction of which brought on the sickness and death of the persons they represented. It was a custom in the time of Catharine de' Medici to make such figures of wax, and melt them slowly before the fire or stab them with needles, in order to bring suffering to enemies. This operation was called putting a spell upon them. We may also mention the opinion of the earlier Christian writers, who believed, according to Draper, that painting and sculpture were interdicted in the Scriptures, and were consequently evil arts. It may be questioned if this opinion did not have its roots in the idea of primitive peoples that the art of drawing was an instrument of sorcery, by means of which one acquired the power to act upon a person. Musulmans still have a horror of images, and the Koran forbids having one's portrait made and possessing any image at all.

We would not exhaust this evidence if we did not cite all the facts that go to prove that, in the mind of primitive man, it was sufficient to possess anything—a piece of the garment, hair, a bit of a nail—that had belonged to a person to have power to act upon him and do him harm. The belief in the efficacy of this means is still so strong among some backward peoples, that persons who have any reason to distrust others hide their clothes so that they shall not be robbed of any part of them. Others, when they cut their hair or nails, put the cut parts on the roofs of their houses or bury them in the ground. So peasants in some countries bury the teeth which they pull from themselves.

We should add, to complete the picture, that writing to the savage enjoys the same magic power as drawing. This is easily understood when we recollect that writing by figures preceded writing by letters or any conventional signs, and is still met among some savage tribes. In these-writings by figures, the fact that the man or animal represented is under the influence of an evil lot is indicated by an arrow directed from the mouth toward the heart. A sign of this kind is considered equivalent to a real possession of the animal or person represented.

We could hardly give more convincing proofs of the special significance attributed by the savage to drawing, regarded by him as an instrument of power over another; and while the examples which we have just brought together relate chiefly to man, we may assume logically that the same process—that is, a figured representation of animals—plays a like part in the struggle of the savage against his natural enemies. Other facts exist confirmatory of this hypothesis.

According to Mr. Tanner, the North American Indians, to assure success in their hunting expeditions, made rude drawings of the animal they were pursuing, and stabbed them in the region of the heart, under the conviction that they would thereby obtain power over the desired game. Taylor relates, according to an old observer among the Australians, that the natives, in one of their festival dances, construct a figure of the kangaroo with plants, in order that they may become masters of the real kangaroos of the forest. An Algonkin Indian, going out to kill an animal, hangs up a figure of it in his lodge; then, after giving it due warning, shoots an arrow at it. If the arrow hits, the animal will be killed. If a hunter, having touched a sorcerer's rod with his arrow, succeeded in hitting the track of the animal with the arrow, it would be stopped and held till the hunter could come up to it. The same object could be attained by drawing the figure of the animal on a piece of wood and addressing suitable prayers to the image.

Such was the function of drawing at its origin. An Indian song admirably explains this function, in the words "My drawing has made a god of me!" Faith could hardly be more vigorously expressed in the power of the art of drawing as an instrument by the aid of which primitive man obtained a supernatural power over his enemy or his game. Regarding the works of the cave men in the light of these facts, we perceive that the purpose that inspired them had few points in common with the sense of the beautiful or the tendency to imitation; and it is clear that if there existed in the mind of the primitive man a material relation between a being and its shadow or its image, that man thought that the same relation was preserved between the being and its image when transferred to any object whatever. The purpose to be reached was to possess the shadow of the coveted object, and the only means of accomplishing it was to fix upon something or another the silhouette of that shadow.

This, in our opinion, was the origin of drawing, and, consequently, of painting. It is worthy of remark that all works of this kind derived from the embryonic period of the arts of design betray the same lack of proportion and absence of symmetry characteristic of the silhouettes of shadows. The uniform impression given by the drawings is that they relate, not to the objects themselves, but to their shadows. It is further interesting to note that some contemporary savages, some Australians, for example, are still incapable of grasping the meaning of exact images, while they readily comprehend a crude, disproportioned drawing. Thus, to give them an idea of a man, you have to draw him with a very large head; a feature with which precisely corresponds a drawing representing a fisherman that has been found in a cave in France. He has a greatly reduced body, but his hand, armed with an enormous harpoon, is the hand of a giant.

In his struggle with surrounding Nature, a struggle of which he cannot form an exact conception, primitive man had especial need to possess every means that could give him confidence in victory. In starting for the hunt he took with him, as the North American Indian does now, and as some players in our most civilized circles do under another form, the fetich that would insure success—that of an image of the animal to be killed. By engraving on the handle of his knife the image of a reindeer or some other animal, he did not think of ornamenting his weapon, but of exerting some magic power over his prey. And his belief in this mysterious power, by giving him boldness, energy, and sureness of movements, would often procure him success. Confidence does thus in all things. Just like the modern savage, the cave man would believe that the greater the resemblance between the image and the animal, the greater also would be the chance of acting upon the animal. Hence the care that was applied to the reproduction of the animals especially coveted and with which the contest would be hardest; and hence those perfect designs of the reindeer, that magnificent game of our ancestors.

Very different are the characteristics of the drawings of human forms; and, to account for these differences, we should consider the fact that all the archæological data relative to the epoch of the reindeer testify that the disposition of the man of that age was pacific. Broca calls these men "peaceful hunters" and attributes a gentle character to them. He remarks that an examination of their arsenal very rarely brings out warlike arms, and that we can thus satisfy ourselves of their peaceful character. The Belgian archæologist, M. Dupont, observes that the cave-dwellers of his country had no idea of war. And, if we have a right to compare the existing savage with primitive man, we find that the Eskimo, who is nearest like him, is quiet and peaceful. The Eskimo whom Ross met on the shores of Baffin's Bay could not be made to understand what war is, and possessed no warlike weapons. While, then, we may believe that the cave men rarely raised their hands against one another, it nevertheless remains determined that they waged a bitter and relentless war against animals. Hence they rarely had occasion to exercise themselves in drawing the human form; and hence the imperfect character of their human images as compared with those of animals. As to the forms of plants, it may be remarked that the boreal flora of that epoch, not being at all threatening, could furnish little food for superstition; and no drawings of plants are found in the caves.

In short, the condition of the art of drawing with primitive man seems to be in complete harmony with the meaning which we have attributed to drawing itself, of its being inspired by belief in the existence of a material relation between a being and its image and in the possibility of acting on the first through the second. Consequently, the principle of painting cannot be found in a natural tendency of primitive man to the artificial imitation of living Nature, but seems rather to be derived from the desire of subjecting that Nature to its needs, and of subjugating it. In the course of its progressive improvements, the art of drawing has gradually lost its primitive significance and original meaning, till it has become what it is now. It does not differ much, however, from what it was originally; for, while the primitive man expected to reach the living being in its image, it is still life which the civilized man seeks today in works of art.